Academic Festival Overture
and Tragic Overture

From the Breitkopf & Härtel Complete Works Edition
Edited by Hans Gál

 DATE DUE

Johannes Brahms

DOVER PUBLICATIONS, INC.
Mineola, New York

CONTENTS

Academic Festival Overture, Op. 80 . . . . **1**
*Composed in 1880 on the occasion of Brahms's honorary doctorate from
the University of Breslau (11 March 1879) and dedicated to the University*

Tragic Overture, Op. 81 . . . . **37**
Composed in 1880, revised in 1881

GLOSSARY OF INSTRUMENT NAMES

Becken, cymbals / *Bratsche*, violas / *Fagotte*, bassoons / *große Flöten*,
flutes / *Hörner*, horns / *Klarinetten*, clarinets / *kleine Flöte*, piccolo /
Kontrabaß, string bass / *Kontrafagott*, contrabassoon / *Oboen*,
oboes / *Pauken*, timpani / *Posaune*, trombones / *Triangel*, triangle /
Trompeten, trumpets / Tuba / *Violine*, violins / *Violoncell*, cellos

Copyright

Bibliographical Note

This Dover edition, first published in 2000, is a republication of two works
in Volume 3: "Ouvertüren und Variationen für Orchester" of *Johannes
Brahms, Sämtliche Werke / Ausgabe der Gesellschaft der Musikfreunde in Wien*,
originally published by Breitkopf & Härtel, Leipzig, n.d. [1926–7]. The
glossary of instrument names is newly added.

International Standard Book Number: 0-486-41176-1

Manufactured in the United States of America
Dover Publications, Inc., 31 East 2nd Street, Mineola, N.Y. 11501

Academic Festival Overture
Op. 80

1

L'istesso tempo, un poco maestoso

235

243

279

290

301

364

381

388

394

397

Tragic Overture

Op. 81